WHAT'S IT LIKE TO BE A...? BUILDER

Elizabeth Dowen   Lisa Thompson

First published in the UK 2008 by
A & C Black Publishing Ltd
38 Soho Square
London
W1D 3HB
www.acblack.com

Copyright © 2008 Blake Publishing
Published 2007 by Black Education Pty Ltd, Australia

ISBN: 978-1-4081-0508-5

A CIP catalogue record for this book is available from the British Library.

Written by Lisa Thompson and Elizabeth Dowen
Publisher: Katy Pike
Series Editor: Eve Tonelli
Cover Design: Terry Woodley
Designers: Debra Brown, Cliff Watt
Printed in China by South China Printing Co. Ltd.

Cover image © Dwight Smith/Shutterstock

Illustration credits: p33 (m), p36 (t) (aap)

This book is produced using paper made from wood grown in managed,
sustainable forests. It is natural, renewable and recyclable. The logging and
manufacturing processes conform to the environmental regulations of the
country of origin.

All the Internet addresses given in this book were correct at the time of
going to press. The author and publishers regret any inconvenience caused
if addresses have changed or sites have ceased to exist, but can accept no
responsibility for any such changes.

Contents

Working in construction

Choosing a career in construction is a very clever move! You won't be going it alone – thousands of people enter the industry each year in the UK.

No matter which job you choose within the construction industry, your work may be admired for years to come.

New houses, commercial properties and government building projects (like the Olympics in 2012) all mean that there are many different construction jobs around in the UK, at all levels.

our building plans

DIDYOUKNOW?

SYDNEY OPERA HOUSE

The Sydney Opera House took 16 years to build. There are over one million white granite tiles on its roofs.

ensuring first row of bricks are level

DID YOU KNOW?

Licensed to build
A builder must have a licence to do most building jobs.

Men's work?

Women account for only 1% of the workforce and most are in professional posts but the government plans to spend around £20 million on training women construction workers in time for the olympics.

SIDE ELEVATION

It's estimated that by 2010, nearly a quarter of a million more construction workers will be needed – both skilled workers and managers. The industry is expected to grow 2-3% in the next 5 years. There are particular shortages in craft trades such as plumbing, plastering, joinery and carpentry.

Most construction jobs are with small companies employing less than 10 workers.

Breaking up an old patio with a jack-hammer is easy.

Scaffolding allows easy access to the roof.

DID YOU KNOW?

Before 2010, the Government plans to spend £76 billion on housing, roads, schools and hospitals.

WHAT ARE THE JOBS?

The construction industry employs people at all levels. Jobs are available in over 35 occupations.

Typical jobs include:

Bricklayer

Plumber

Carpenter

Painter and Decorator

Joiner

Electrician

Plasterer

Floor layer

Roofer

Scaffolder

Workers are often trained in more than one construction occupation. This is called multi-skilling. Construction is becoming more technical and workers need to develop their skills.

Welcome to the Building Site

There are three things you will always find on a building site – hard work, dirt and noise.

The building site is a hive of activity. People are hard at work with power tools – like power saws and drills. Overhead, a crane manoeuvres huge steel beams into place. A pneumatic drill jerks around in the dirt. An electrician threads cables through a hole in a new wall. Plans and measurements are checked and rechecked.

Health and safety is so important on building sites. No-one is allowed on site without the right safety gear and training.

The construction industry in Britain is said to be one of the safest in Europe but construction work can be dangerous. Accidents can happen when getting to work, while walking across building sites, handling work materials or moving around the workplace.

Labourers, Technicians or Professionals?

Most workers in construction are skilled, but some of the heavy work on building sites does not require particular skills. This is called labouring.

Labouring jobs can pay well, but are often only temporary. Sometimes there is no work in bad weather. You need to be fit and strong, which means that you will find it harder to get jobs as you get older. For better prospects it's a good idea to train for a skilled trade.

Technician work specialises in design, surveying, costing, testing and managing. There are civil engineering technicians, building technicians and architectural technicians.

Professional jobs may deal with the construction of buildings and structures, services (such as heating, water and sewerage systems) or the finance and logistics of projects.

Jobs include:
- Architect
- Project or contract manager
- Building control officer
- Waste management engineer
- Civil engineer
- Building and quantity surveyor
- Structural engineer

Employers say that there is a real shortage of these things:

- technical and practical skills
- problem solving abilities
- good communication
- customer service
- team working skills

What's the future?

Multi-skilling is growing in importance.

Competition for places on courses for skilled trades, particularly plumbing, is very strong.

Permanent jobs are more difficult to fill than contract jobs.

Civil engineering recruitment hotspots in the UK include the North West and North East for operatives and engineers.

The use of new materials and changing methods of building will affect how the construction industry operates.

Level	Type of job	Qualifications examples
1 few or no qualifications	Operative Labourer on site	OSAT (On Site Assessment and Training)
2 / 3 Craft level	Joiner Bricklayer Plumber Plasterer Painter and Decorator	Train with an employer through an Apprenticeship, leading to NVQ level 2, or an Advanced Apprenticeship, leading to NVQ level 3. Apprenticeships are available through a range of training providers. NVQ 2 in individual skill areas - craft level May go on to take advanced and specialist training - NVQ 3, Certificates of Competence such as CORGI Apprenticeship (mostly for 16-19s)
3 / 4 Technician level	Architectural technician Building service technician Quantity surveying technician	NVQ 3 in individual skill areas - Technician level Advanced Apprenticeship (mostly for 16-19s) National Certificate National Diploma in the Built Environment Foundation Degree Higher National Certificate (HNC)
4 / 5 Professional level	Quantity surveyor Building manager Architect Civil Engineer	Higher National Diploma (HND) Degree plus membership of professional bodies Continuous professional development

Useful school subjects for becoming a builder:

- maths — to make quick calculations
- technical drawing — to read construction plans and be able to explain them to other people
- woodwork — to understand building materials and tools

What are employers looking for?

People who are:

- Practical
- Qualified in practical or technical skills
- Multi-skilled
- Numerate, literate and understand instructions
- Able to work at heights
- Reasonably strong (for site workers)
- Aware of health and safety

People who like:

- Team working
- Solving problems
- Working outdoors and in enclosed spaces
- Working around the country
- Keeping up with new developments

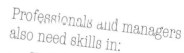

Professionals and managers also need skills in:

- High level technical or practical work
- Management
- Project management
- Communication and customer handling
- Business finance
- 'Professional' IT packages

CRAFT JOBS

These are the well-known skilled trades, such as bricklaying, plumbing and roofing. In many of these jobs, you work outside - enjoyable in the summer maybe, but not so good when the weather's bad! If you have a trade with scope for indoor work, your earnings are less affected by the weather.

BRICKLAYERS

Trained bricklayers make this job look simple. In fact, there's a lot more to it than you might think. As well as learning the skills of laying bricks (including making arches and decorative effects), bricklayers learn about the types of bricks and cements, safe methods of working and so on.

To be a bricklayer you must be reasonably fit and strong and able to lift heavy weights. You also need to:

- be prepared to work outdoors
- be safety-conscious
- work quickly but accurately using practical skills
- understand architectural plans and drawings
- be able to climb ladders and work at heights
- like working both in a team and on your own
- travel, sometimes spending time away from home.
- A driving licence is useful.

Much of a bricklayer's work is done out of doors. It can be dirty work! In the summer, bricklayers often work longer hours but in winter bad weather can stop to work altogether.

No boots
No job

CARPENTERS AND JOINERS

All sorts of woodwork involve reading drawings and plans, knowing about types of wood and working very accurately. Carpenters and joiners work mostly on building sites and in workshops. Tasks include:

- making wooden structures to shape concrete as it sets
- cutting and fixing joists, wooden partitions and panelling
- laying floorboards
- making and fixing doors, window frames, stairs, kitchen units and skirting
- erecting roof timbers.

ELECTRICIANS need to

be good at practical work and theory. The work may range from rewiring a house to a complex job like installing the electrical supply in a factory.

SCAFFOLDERS

You need a good head for heights! Putting up and taking down scaffolding on building projects is complicated. It must be done carefully, as the safety of many workers depends on it. Scaffolding poles are heavy, so the work is physically hard.

DIDYOUKNOW?

You may travel quite a way to work on a big project or to do specialist work on listed buildings. This may mean living away from home for a time, either in this country or abroad.

13

PLUMBERS - use mostly plastic and copper piping, with some brasswork for special appliances. Plumbing in large buildings can be very complicated. Home central heating needs a lot of pipework. Sometimes plumbers are also registered gas fitters as they use similar skills.

CEILING FIXERS - use materials such as metal, timber or tiles for suspended ceilings. New ceilings are often put up by the builder and finished by the plasterer, but some ceilings, for example, in large buildings, need specialist skills.

GLAZIERS - may work on site, cutting and fitting large plate glass windows and doors . Also they may work in a workshop, preparing glass for fitting by builders or home DIY making and fitting double glazing.

ROOFERS - need a good head for heights and must follow safety rules. They all work outdoors, of course. Roofers usually specialise in slating and tiling, sheeting and cladding or built-up felt roofing.

PLASTERERS - need to work very quickly and neatly. Solid plastering involves applying a wet finish to walls and other surfaces in buildings. Fibrous plasterers make ornamental mouldings. Plasterers have to know about the materials they use and learn how to estimate the quantities needed for jobs.

DRY-LINING OPERATIVES

- put up the finished surfaces of interior walls which are not being plastered - using materials like plasterboard. You need to be accurate, good at calculating and fit.

WALL AND FLOOR TILLERS - need

to know how to measure and cut tiles, choose the right adhesives for the job, and estimate the quantities required. Some tillers specialise in mosaic and other tiles as wall decorations.

FLOORLAYERS – Vinyl flooring and

wood effect flooring are examples of the wide range of other materials used as floor covering. Each must be handled differently using special adhesives and methods of laying. Floorlayers may work for contractors, or for flooring manufacturers and carpet and flooring shops providing service for customers.

PAINTERS AND DECORATORS

- have to learn to use different skills and materials. Lots of different decorative finishes are used, mostly paint and wallpaper. Preparing surfaces to be decorated is an important part of the work.

Painters and decorators have to learn how to use all types of brushes and rollers, and perhaps mechanical hand tools like blow torches and spray-painting equipment. It takes time to become really skilled at painting and decorating techniques. You need to be fast, clean and accurate.

Painters and decorators paint new buildings inside and out and wallpaper. They also work on older buildings, redecorating and repainting interiors and exteriors to a professional standard. They have to know how to prepare and treat different surfaces ready for painting or decorating.

INSULATION, DAMP-PROOF COURSING

Some firms put down loft insulation, inject cavity wall insulation or damp-proof walls. Training is normally on the job. You need to understand the materials and wear protective clothing. Laggers use insulating material, such as fibreglass, cork or foam, to cover pipes and boilers to prevent heat loss. There is some risk of allergy from the materials used, and you must be able to cope with heights.

STONEMASONS

A well-qualified stonemason is in great demand by cathedrals, conservation societies and the like, to repair damage done to historical buildings by the years and the weather. This kind of restoration work takes a lot of time, but the results are very satisfying.

Most stonemasons work on new buildings or specialise as a monumental or memorial mason, making and carving gravestones. A monumental mason is a banker, carver, fixer and letter sculptor.

Banker masons work mainly in a workshop where conditions can be noisy and dusty. They wear special safety equipment to protect their ears and eyes.

Fixer masons work on site in different locations, sometimes away from home. They have to work in all weathers, very often on scaffolding.

PLANT WORKERS

On construction sites, plant operators drive and operate a wide range of heavy equipment - diggers, trucks and cranes. Safety is a top priority. Plant mechanics do the very important job of keeping the equipment running smoothly. A plant which is out of action means lost time and, therefore, money!

ASPHALTERS - lay asphalt on drives, car parks, playgrounds, road surfaces and so on. Some firms are large contractors which tender for government contracts, but others may only employ one or two people who do small domestic jobs. Asphalting is hard physical work, done in all weathers.

FENCE ERECTORS - put up structures of wire, wood and so on to enclose or separate areas. The work may involve reading plans, and other building jobs such as preparing the site, levelling ground and concreting. They need to be skilled in a range of building tasks.

SHOPFITTERS - choose, cut and shape materials such as glass, plastic, metal or wood to make the interiors of shops, banks, hotels and so on. They need to measure, calculate and work accurately, using a variety of skills and a wide range of tools.

STEEPLEJACKS - work on church steeples and other high buildings, like factory chimneys. Their work includes safety inspections, repair work and maintenance, installing lightning conductors, and demolition. Basic requirements are a good head for heights and a responsible attitude to safety.

DEMOLITION WORKERS - remove unwanted buildings and clear sites. They use a range of machines and tools, and even explosives. Demolition workers have to be very safety-conscious - the minimum age is 18. The work calls for lots of stamina and is very dusty, so protective clothing is normally worn.

PROFESSIONAL ROLES

These jobs require at least one degree and professional accreditation. They are very competitive so you are aiming high and need to be prepared to work hard!

Surveyors

Surveying involves measuring, valuing, managing and developing all types of buildings and land, including rocks and minerals and even the seabed.

Surveyors must have:
- practical problem-solving skills
- an analytical and logical approach to their work
- some expertise in technical, legal and financial matters
- good communication and team skills.

Architects and architectural technicians

Architecture means designing new buildings, and restoring and converting buildings and other structures.

Architects specialise in design work.

Architectural technologists

specialise in the technical design and specifications of buildings, for example, producing technical instructions and working drawings for builders.

Architectural technicians

assist in project development, computer-aided design (CAD) and tendering. You need to:

- be creative with the ability to visualise in three dimensions
- have good team skills
- have good problem-solving and numerical skills
- have the ability to work accurately and methodically
- be a good communicator - you will have a lot of contact with clients, contractors and other professionals.

Civil or structural engineers

Working on civil and structural engineering projects like new bridges, roads or industrial plants is a team effort. Engineers have responsibility for design and research and for construction work. The job is a mixture of office- and site-based, working alongside building or maintenance contractors.

DID YOU KNOW?

You can't call yourself an architect unless you are registered with the Architects Registration Board (ARB). There are currently 25 full- and part-time architectural technology degree courses in the UK accredited by the Chartered Institute of Architectural Technologists (CIAT), the professional body.

STRUCTURAL ELEMENTS

The structural elements of a building are the foundation, frame and walls. They hold the building together. Other elements, such as roof tiles and windows, only enclose or decorate a building. Structural elements cannot be removed without damaging the strength and shape of the building.

columns to support the roof

DID YOU KNOW?

THE WORLD'S OLDEST BUILDING

Newgrange, a burial chamber built in Ireland over 5 000 years ago, is the world's oldest existing building. It is more than 500 years older than the Great Pyramid of Giza in Egypt, and predates Stonehenge in Britain by about 1 000 years. Constructed in an age when people had only wood and stone to work with its roof remains intact to this day. It is also regarded as the oldest observatory in the world, purposely built to align with the rising sun at midwinter.

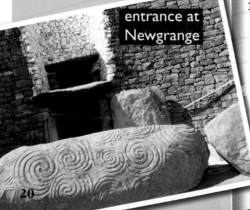
entrance at Newgrange

LOAD

Structures are built to withstand certain loads. The weight of a building itself is called the **dead load** — it doesn't move or change. The weight of objects that go in and out of a building (people, furniture, machinery) is called the **live load** — it moves and changes depending on what is going on in the building. A builder must understand which materials and building techniques are appropriate for the structure's live load.

bridge

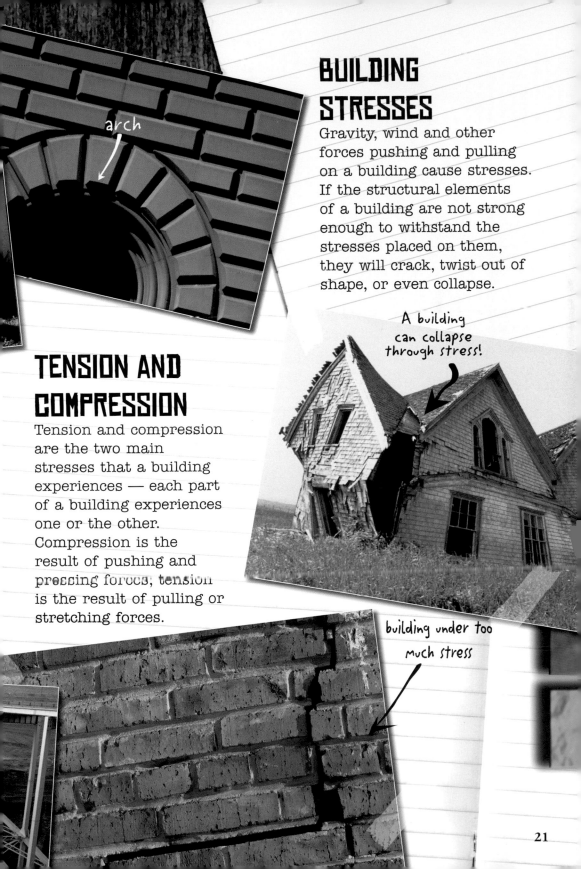

arch

BUILDING STRESSES

Gravity, wind and other forces pushing and pulling on a building cause stresses. If the structural elements of a building are not strong enough to withstand the stresses placed on them, they will crack, twist out of shape, or even collapse.

A building can collapse through stress!

TENSION AND COMPRESSION

Tension and compression are the two main stresses that a building experiences — each part of a building experiences one or the other. Compression is the result of pushing and pressing forces; tension is the result of pulling or stretching forces.

building under too much stress

21

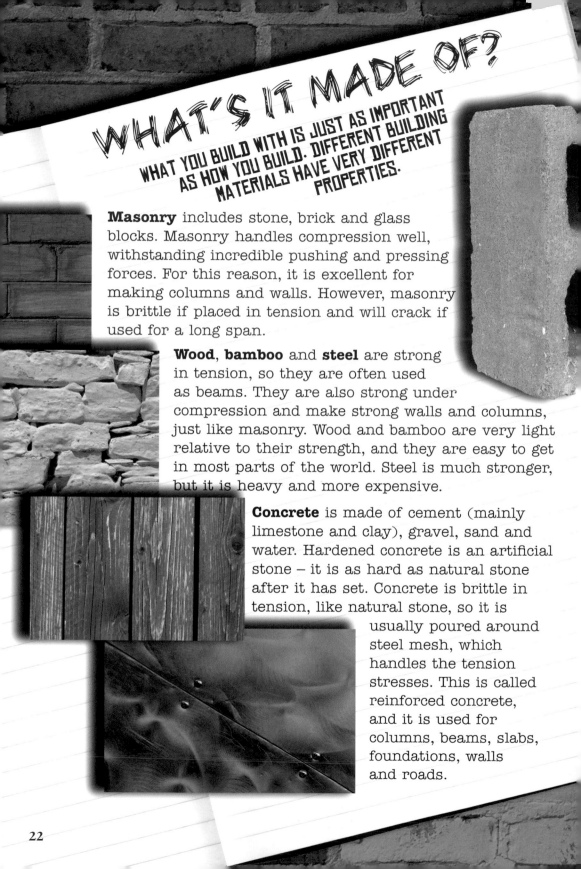

WHAT'S IT MADE OF?

WHAT YOU BUILD WITH IS JUST AS IMPORTANT AS HOW YOU BUILD. DIFFERENT BUILDING MATERIALS HAVE VERY DIFFERENT PROPERTIES.

Masonry includes stone, brick and glass blocks. Masonry handles compression well, withstanding incredible pushing and pressing forces. For this reason, it is excellent for making columns and walls. However, masonry is brittle if placed in tension and will crack if used for a long span.

Wood, **bamboo** and **steel** are strong in tension, so they are often used as beams. They are also strong under compression and make strong walls and columns, just like masonry. Wood and bamboo are very light relative to their strength, and they are easy to get in most parts of the world. Steel is much stronger, but it is heavy and more expensive.

Concrete is made of cement (mainly limestone and clay), gravel, sand and water. Hardened concrete is an artificial stone – it is as hard as natural stone after it has set. Concrete is brittle in tension, like natural stone, so it is usually poured around steel mesh, which handles the tension stresses. This is called reinforced concrete, and it is used for columns, beams, slabs, foundations, walls and roads.

Material	Pros	Cons	Uses
Brick	Cheap, and strong in compression.	Heavy, and weak in tension.	Walls, tunnels, domes.
Wood	Cheap, lightweight and moderately strong in compression and tension. A renewable resource.	Rots, swells and burns easily. Can be eaten by termites.	Floors, and framing for walls, windows and roofs. Cladding for walls and roofs.
Steel	Strong in compression and tension. One of the strongest construction materials.	Rusts, and loses strength in extremely high temperatures.	Trusses, beams and columns. Cables in suspension bridges.
Reinforced concrete	Strong in compression and tension. Cheap, fireproof and weatherproof. Moulds to any shape.	Can crack as it cools and hardens. Steel reinforcing can rust and crack the concrete.	Bridges, foundations, dams, domes, beams and columns.

THE B, C AND D OF BUILDING

b=BEAM

A beam is a horizontal structural element that spans an opening, supported at both ends by walls or columns. There are beams in almost every building, from small houses to huge skyscrapers. When beams and columns are the main feature of a building, it is called a "post and beam" structure.

beam

post

Steel beams can span large areas.

a basic post and beam structure

C=CANTILEVER

A cantilever is like a beam but it is only supported at one end. A load on the building balances the weight of the part that projects out into space. Cantilevers are common in buildings, bridges, and even the wings of planes.

Many balconies are cantilevers — the balcony does not fall because it extends back into the building

BUILDING

support

Huge stone beams were lifted four metres above the ground to create Stonehenge 3 500 years ago.

DOME

arch

The glass and steel dome above the Reichstag building in Berlin, Germany, allows people to see parliament in action.

d = DOME

A dome is the shape formed by a series of arches sitting on a circular base. All the surfaces of a dome are curved. Domes are very strong and are often built as roofs above round or square spaces.

Each floor of the Whitney Museum in New York is a cantilever above the one below.

Saint Basil's Cathedral in Moscow, Russia, has many 'onion' domes.

BUILT TO LAST
TECHNIQUES FOR MAKING STRONG STRUCTURES

Thick beams are less likely to bend than thin beams. They also absorb vibration, making a structure stronger and more rigid.

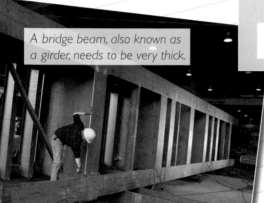

A bridge beam, also known as a girder, needs to be very thick.

Cross-bracing adds strength to lightweight structures.

Cross-bracing is an excellent way to stiffen a structure. Diagonal braces squeeze together and resist lateral (sideways) forces on the structure.

Concrete pillars or piles support structures built on soft soil. They are sunk deep into the earth until they rest on hard, solid soil or rock, which keeps the structure stable above ground.

Concrete pillars will support this bridge.

DIDYOUKNOW?

THE PENTAGON

The Pentagon in the United States of America is one of the world's largest buildings in terms of floor area. It houses approximately 26,000 employees. It has five sides, five floors above ground (plus two basement levels), and five ring corridors per floor with a total of 28 km of corridors. It takes 15-20 minutes to walk around the Pentagon once.

These piles must support the weight of the jetty and resist the force of waves and wind.

Cross-bracing of cranes keeps them rigid under heavy loads and high winds.

Shear walls are heavy, solid vertical walls of reinforced concrete or masonry. They give a building strength and stiffness. Shear walls resist lateral forces, such as those caused by wind and earthquakes.

Most structures use a combination of thick and thin beams.

Concrete will be poured around the steel reinforcing to add another storey to this building.

Walls can be pre-made and then dropped into position.

5 STEPS TO BUILDING A HOUSE

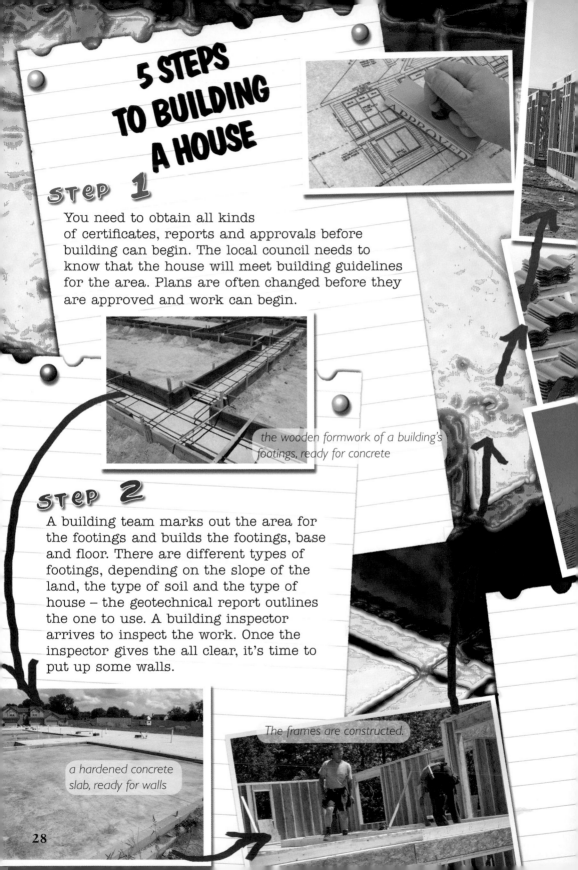

STEP 1

You need to obtain all kinds of certificates, reports and approvals before building can begin. The local council needs to know that the house will meet building guidelines for the area. Plans are often changed before they are approved and work can begin.

the wooden formwork of a building's footings, ready for concrete

STEP 2

A building team marks out the area for the footings and builds the footings, base and floor. There are different types of footings, depending on the slope of the land, the type of soil and the type of house – the geotechnical report outlines the one to use. A building inspector arrives to inspect the work. Once the inspector gives the all clear, it's time to put up some walls.

a hardened concrete slab, ready for walls

The frames are constructed.

wall framing

roof trusses

DIDYOUKNOW?

KEEPING YOUR BALANCE
For a stable ladder, the distance from the base of an extension ladder to the wall should be one-quarter of the ladder's extended length.

Roof tiles are laid over wooden battens.

Electricians run wiring through a building's wooden frame.

Plasterboard walls are patched before being sealed and painted.

STEP 4

The plumber and the electrician arrive to install plumbing and electrical fittings; when the internal walls are finished, they will return to finish the job. The builders and carpenters fit external and internal wall linings, windows, doors, cupboards and mouldings.

STEP 3

The wall frames are either delivered ready-made (pre-cut and even pre-nailed) or are made on site. The walls are erected, followed by the ready-made roof framing (trusses). Once the frame of the house is up, the building inspector returns to check the work again.
When it has passed inspection, roofing contractors arrive to cover the roof.

STEP 5

The plumber and the electrician finish up, and the painters take over. After a final tidy-up of the site, it's time for the owners to move in!

selecting colour for painting

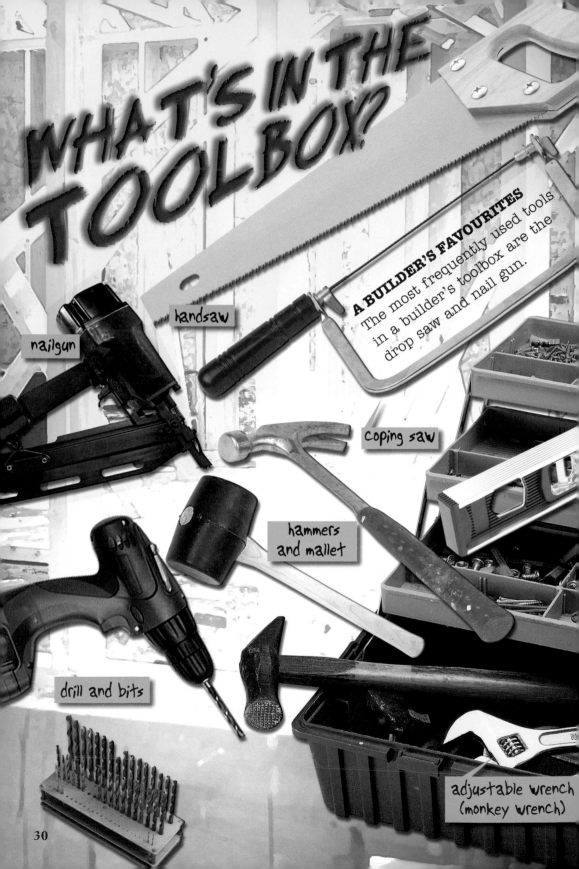

WHAT'S IN THE TOOLBOX?

A BUILDER'S FAVOURITES
The most frequently used tools in a builder's toolbox are the drop saw and nail gun.

nailgun

handsaw

coping saw

hammers and mallet

drill and bits

adjustable wrench (monkey wrench)

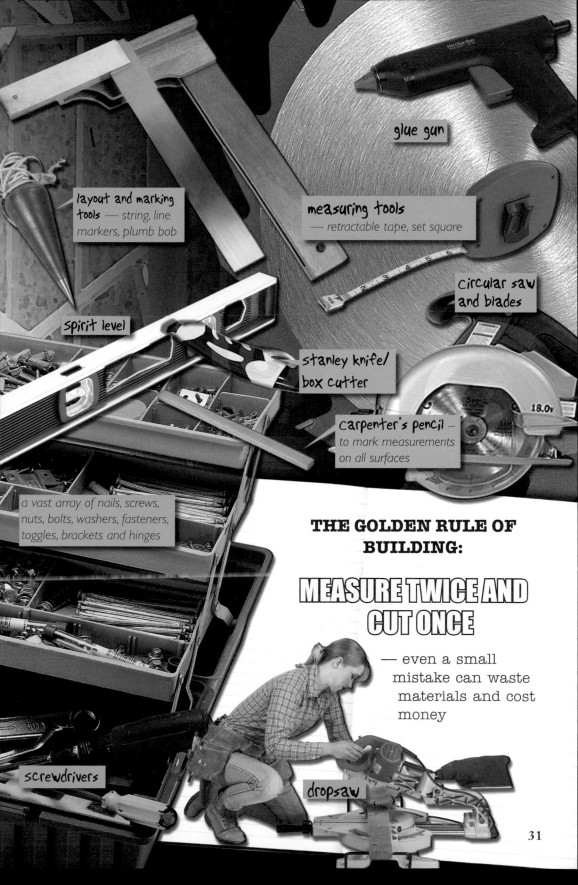

glue gun

layout and marking tools — string, line markers, plumb bob

measuring tools — retractable tape, set square

circular saw and blades

spirit level

stanley knife/ box cutter

carpenter's pencil — to mark measurements on all surfaces

a vast array of nails, screws, nuts, bolts, washers, fasteners, toggles, brackets and hinges

18.0v

THE GOLDEN RULE OF BUILDING:

MEASURE TWICE AND CUT ONCE

— even a small mistake can waste materials and cost money

screwdrivers

dropsaw

FAMOUS BUILDERS IN HISTORY

KING SNEFRU (AROUND 2613–2589 BC)

The ancient Egyptians built pyramids because they believed that life originated from mounds, so burying a king inside a pyramid meant that he would live forever. King Snefru's experiments in building pyramids influenced the building of the great pyramids at Giza. His construction team shifted around 3.5 million cubic metres of stone, and built the first true pyramid in Egypt, the Red Pyramid.

The building teams that worked on the Red Pyramid wrote their names on some of the blocks in red paint — such as the Green Gang and the Western Gang.

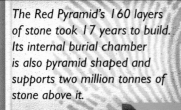

The Red Pyramid's 160 layers of stone took 17 years to build. Its internal burial chamber is also pyramid shaped and supports two million tonnes of stone above it.

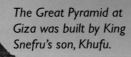

The Great Pyramid at Giza was built by King Snefru's son, Khufu.

arch

THE ANCIENT ROMANS

Perhaps more than any other civilisation, the Romans are famous for their incredible constructions. Working with stone, bricks, concrete and wood, they built the Colosseum in Rome, and the Hagia Sophia in what is now Instanbul, Turkey. They also built aqueducts to carry water across great distances.

Roman aquaduct

DIDYOUKNOW?

VISIBLE FROM SPACE?

One of the modern myths about the Great Wall of China is that it is the only man-made structure visible from space. In fact, the Great Wall is no wider than an airport runway, and is the same color as the countryside surrounding it, making it almost impossible to see. However, it can be seen from space when conditions are perfect – with the help of binoculars!

Hagia Sophia

FAMOUS BUILDERS IN HISTORY

Alexandre Gustave Eiffel (1832–1923)

Eiffel was a French engineer and architect who loved maths and science. He had a great understanding of how metals could be used in building —how they could be shaped and what stresses they could handle. His most famous project was the Eiffel Tower, built for the 1889 World Fair in Paris. It was the tallest building in the world for 40 years. Eiffel also designed the internal supporting structure of the Statue of Liberty, a gift from France to the United States of America.

The Eiffel Tower took two years to build and contains 2.5 million rivets.

The Eiffel Tower

A viewing platform in Liberty's crown is reached via an internal stairway.

POSTES

REPUBLIQUE FRANC

The curved panels of the Guggenheim Museum were cut by robot-controlled lasers.

The Guggenheim Museum
Bilbao, Spain

Guggenheim ceiling

Frank Gehry (1929–)

Gehry is an American architect whose buildings often look like sculptures. Using the latest computer-aided design programs, Gehry designs buildings that resemble fish, ships, or crumpled pieces of paper. His most famous building is the Guggenheim Museum in Bilbao, Spain. Covered in titanium panels as thin as paper, the exterior of the museum has no flat surfaces!

In the commercial construction industry, builders and carpenters can work on all kinds of projects, such as office buildings, apartments, bridges, tunnels, libraries, dams and sports stadiums.

A builder on a commercial construction site works with other specialised team members, like civil engineers, construction managers, architects, subcontractors, property developers and construction crews.

Can a builder become a construction manager?

Yes! With extra training and lots of experience on building sites, builders can become construction managers. They coordinate the entire construction process, from initial planning through to the final coat of paint.

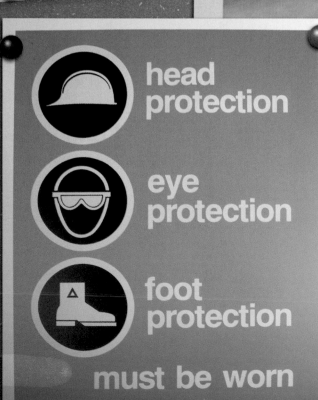

head protection

eye protection

foot protection

must be worn

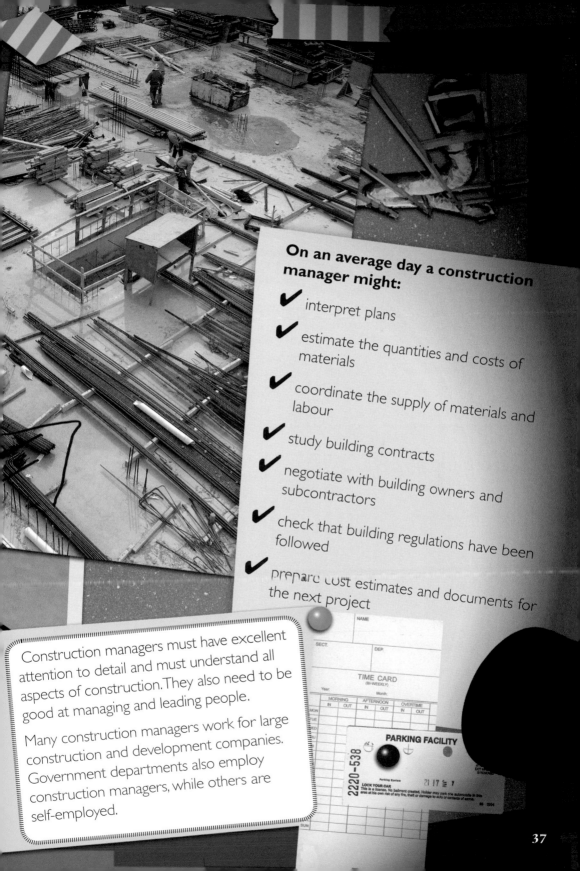

On an average day a construction manager might:

✔ interpret plans

✔ estimate the quantities and costs of materials

✔ coordinate the supply of materials and labour

✔ study building contracts

✔ negotiate with building owners and subcontractors

✔ check that building regulations have been followed

✔ prepare cost estimates and documents for the next project

Construction managers must have excellent attention to detail and must understand all aspects of construction. They also need to be good at managing and leading people.

Many construction managers work for large construction and development companies. Government departments also employ construction managers, while others are self-employed.

Building the world's tallest tower

Construction is underway on the world's tallest building, the Burj Dubai Tower in the United Arab Emirates, due for completion in 2008. It will reach over 700 metres high, nearly 200 metres taller than the current tallest building, the Taipei 101 Tower in Taiwan.

The shape of a desert flower influenced the design of the Burj Dubai Tower. The tower will have 160 floors built around a central core, and the tower's engineers have shaped the building to minimise the effect of wind. It will contain shops, hotels and apartments, and an outdoor swimming pool on the 78th floor. The Burj Dubai Tower will feature the world's fastest elevator, rocketing skyward at 18 metres per second (64 kilometres per hour).

World's top 3 tallest building

1. Name:
   Taipei 101
   Location: Taipei, Taiwan
   Completed: 2004
   Floors: 101
   Height (to spire): 508 metres

3. Name:

Sears Tower
Location: Chicago, USA
Completed: 1974
Floors: 108
Height (to roof):
442 metres

2. Name:

Petronas Towers
Location: Kuala Lumpur, Malaysia
Completed: 1998
Floors: 88
Height (to spire):
452 metres

DECEMBER

30 Wednesday

7:30 AM

I GET THE FIRST PHONE CALL OF THE DAY FROM ONE OF MY SITE MANAGERS. WE DISCUSS SOME MINOR CHANGES TO A JOB AS REQUESTED BY THE CLIENT.

8 AM

I DROP OFF SOME TOOLS TO A TEAM MEMBER WORKING ON A NEW HOUSE. BECAUSE I AM RESPONSIBLE FOR THE SAFETY OF EVERYONE ON SITE, I CHECK THAT SAFETY PROCEDURES ARE BEING FOLLOWED — HARD HATS AND HARNESSES ARE BEING WORN, POWER TOOLS HAVE BEEN CERTIFIED AS SAFE AND EVERYONE ON SITE KNOWS WHERE THE CLOSEST HOSPITAL IS (JUST IN CASE THERE'S AN ACCIDENT).

8:30 AM

NOW I AM IN THE OFFICE AND THERE'S TIME TO REVIEW A JOB QUOTE I'VE BEEN WORKING ON. SOME PRICES FOR STEEL FRAMING CAME THROUGH VIA EMAIL YESTERDAY, SO I INCLUDE THEM IN MY CALCULATIONS OF THE COST PER SQUARE METRE OF BUILDING AREA.

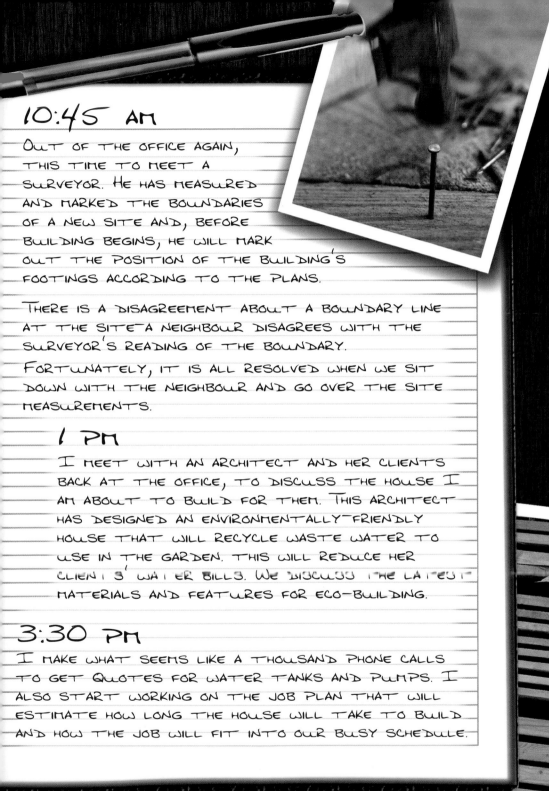

10:45 AM

Out of the office again, this time to meet a surveyor. He has measured and marked the boundaries of a new site and, before building begins, he will mark out the position of the building's footings according to the plans.

There is a disagreement about a boundary line at the site—a neighbour disagrees with the surveyor's reading of the boundary. Fortunately, it is all resolved when we sit down with the neighbour and go over the site measurements.

1 PM

I meet with an architect and her clients back at the office, to discuss the house I am about to build for them. This architect has designed an environmentally-friendly house that will recycle waste water to use in the garden. This will reduce her client's water bills. We discuss the latest materials and features for eco-building.

3:30 PM

I make what seems like a thousand phone calls to get quotes for water tanks and pumps. I also start working on the job plan that will estimate how long the house will take to build and how the job will fit into our busy schedule.

FOLLOW THESE STEPS TO BECOME A BUILDER

There are opportunities at all levels of qualification.

In school:
- A good reference from school or from a work-experience placement can be helpful. Maths, Science, English and Design and Technology are useful GCSE subjects.
- A GCSE in construction and the Built Environment is being piloted in some schools.
- The new Foundation Diploma in Construction and Built Environment (C&BE) Diploma – see page 44 for more details.

After 16:
- Another way for young people to get started in construction is through employer-based training. This means learning both on the job and at a college or training centre, working towards NVQs.

2

- You may train with an employer through an Apprenticeship leading to NVQ level 2, or an Advanced Apprenticeship leading to NVQ level 3. Apprenticeships are available in a wide range of building trades.

- You can also learn construction skills through a full-time college course. Many further education colleges offer courses leading to construction awards (assessed at college) and some courses lead to NVQs. There are other courses, such as BTEC First and National qualifications in construction, which offer a broad-based introduction to the building industry. Courses vary in length.

- The Armed Forces offer training to servicemen and women in many different construction trades.

The new Construction and Built Environment Diploma will teach you practical skills and theoretical and technical knowledge. The C&BE Diploma will begin to be taught in England from September 2008. It will be delivered through schools, colleges and employers.

The Diploma will be easy to recognise and understand, and valuable to employers who appreciate traditional qualifications but who also feel that young people should have broader skills.

The Diploma will have three levels:

• Foundation Level - provides an introduction to the built environment, the factors influencing its design and construction and its impact on people and communities.

• Higher Level - develops and applies a range of skills and knowledge in relation to the design, creation, maintenance and use of the built environment.

• Advanced Level - provides opportunities to analyse, evaluate and explore principles and practices relating to the social, economic and cultural contribution of the built environment and the wider factors influencing the design, creation, maintenance and management of the built environment.

Diplomas will not teach you particular trade training though (bricklayer, plumber or electrician). You need to do an apprenticeship or full-time college course for that.

Ask your school or careers/Connexions adviser for more information.

OPPORTUNITIES FOR BUILDERS IN THE CONSTRUCTION INDUSTRY

Most craftspeople in construction earn around £15-25,000.

Skilled people in shortage areas can earn £40-50,000 a year on major construction projects – but less on a local building site or for a small employer. Technicians and professionals earn salaries comparable to other industries.

Craftspeople can continue their study and training to higher levels, or can move into teaching construction skills.

Many building workers become self-employed.

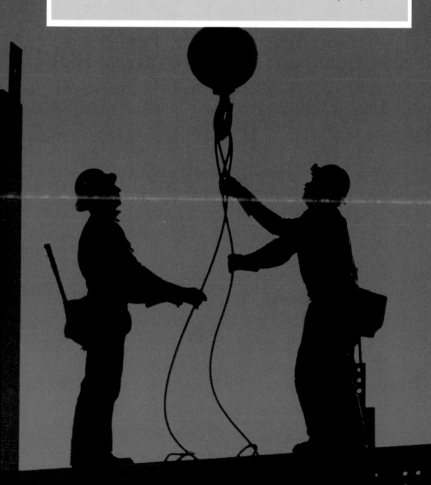

Glossary

apprentice — someone who works for a skilled person, often for a basic wage, in order to learn that person's skills

asphalt— derived from oil, used in surfacing roads or as waterproofing in buildings

beam — a piece of wood, metal or concrete used to support weight in a structure

compression — the stress on a structure from a weight pushing or pressing against it

corrugated — having parallel rows of folds, which look like waves when seen from the edge

cross-bracing — a diagonal structural member used to strengthen a frame

dome — a rounded roof on a building

footing — the part of a foundation that touches the ground

foundation — the lowest, load-bearing part of a building

geotechnician — an engineer who investigates the soil and rock below a building site to determine the type of foundations required

lateral — relating to the sides of an object or to sideways movement

load — the amount of weight carried by a structure or part of a structure

mouldings — a piece of moulded wood, plaster or plastic for decorating a wall, door or window

plumb line — a piece of string with a weight fixed to one end; used to test whether something is vertical

span — the length between two supports, such as columns

stonemason— someone who cuts, prepares and builds with stone

tension — the stress on a structure resulting from stretching

tradespeople — people who work in a trade such as electricians, plumbers, carpenters, etc.

translucent — almost transparent; allowing some light to pass through

trusses — a framework of beams forming a roof

Useful contacts and websites

ConstructionSkills – Tel: 01485 577 577 for details of your local office. Or contact details can be found on the website, along with information about careers, qualifications and Apprenticeships. *www.bconstructive.co.uk*

JTL – Tel: 0800 085 2308. Provides training in electrical and plumbing work. Contact the Centre for details of your local JTL training officer. *www.jtltraining.com*

Women & Manual Trades *www.wamt.org*

Wise (Women into Science, Engineering and Construction) *www.wisecampaign.org.uk*

Stonemasonry courses are listed on local and national course databases, such as *www.learndirect-advice.co.uk*

Chartered Institute of Architectural Technologists (CIAT) Produces **Your Career in Architectural Technology**, which includes a list of courses approved by CIAT and is provided free on request, or can be viewed on their website: *www.ciat.org.uk*

Royal Institute of British Architects (RIBA) Careers information and validated courses can be found on the website: *www.architecture.com*

Institution of Civil Engineers *(ICE)* - *www.ice.org.uk/education*

The Institution of Structural Engineers - *www.istructe.org*

Targetjobs Construction 2008: School Leaver Edition - published by **GTI Specialist Publishers**, may be available in schools, colleges and Connexions/careers centres.

For information about foundation degree, HNC/D and degree courses, refer to higher education reference books and databases, which may be available in Connexions/careers libraries, or view the UCAS website: *www.ucas.com*

www.eclips-online.co.uk gives a full database of all the jobs in the construction industry and entry requirements in detail.

Index